To Mary

Happy Birthday
Lots of Love

John

EDINBURGH

EDINBURGH

PHOTOGRAPHED BY DOUGLAS CORRANCE
WITH CAPTIONS BY W. GORDON SMITH

COLLINS GLASGOW AND LONDON

Published by William Collins Sons and Company Limited

Photographs © Scottish Tourist Board
Text © William Collins Sons and Company Limited

First published 1979
Reprinted 1980
Printed in Great Britain

ISBN 0 00 411143 5

PREFACE

I have been asked why I wanted to do this book on Edinburgh. Not an easy question to answer. I have lived in the city for five years and hardly a day passes but I discover something new to admire: a delicate fanlight in the New Town; a shop with a frontage from the era of elegance unsullied by chrome and plastic. These things give so much pleasure and they are the real Edinburgh. Thankfully, the city has not suffered as badly as some others. Even so, much irreparable damage has already taken place and a halt must be called to this "progress". It is a bit of a cliché to say Edinburgh has character but how else can one describe it. It is this character I have tried to capture and I hope that by doing so I have found a responsive chord in others who think as I do.

DOUGLAS CORRANCE

INTRODUCTION

In the middle of my play "Jock" I have the man himself—he has become a Glaswegian by habit and repute—tell the story of the Edinburgh man's confrontation with St Peter at the pearly gates.

"You were a merchant," says St Peter, consulting his big book.

"Aye," says the Edinburgh man, "and I traded fair and square and I looked after my workers like a father."

"So you did."

"And, as a bailie, I dealt fearlessly with wrongdoers, tempering my judgments with appropriate mercy."

"Aye, so you did, too," says St Peter.

"As a kirk elder I served the Lord in all things and at all times."

St Peter looks in vain for any blemish on the record.

"You've certainly led an honest and exemplary life. Where was it you said you came from?"

"Edinburgh," says the Edinburgh man.

"Well you can come in," says St Peter, throwing open the gates, "but you'll not like it here at all."

The late John Rafferty, doyen of Scottish sport writers, used to say that belonging to Edinburgh, as I do and he did not, was a great affliction because it wasn't something you could have an operation for. Both stories say a lot about the quality of the place and the character of the people.

There are, of course, many Edinburghs, and I belong to them all and they, in an almost mystical sense, belong to me. Lavender and old lace Edinburgh, where mirrors are bracketed outside windows—all the better to see you with, from behind the curtains—where "The Scotsman" used to be ironed flat and crisp every morning. Commercial Edinburgh, where big money is manipulated as if from a suburb of Zurich. Industrial Edinburgh, belching the stink of brewer's mash, and if the wind's in the wrong quarter who smells the abundant wallflower in the city parks? Artistic Edinburgh—lively, fey and a wee bit pretentious. Deprived Edinburgh, where life seems to fester away in suburban ghettoes.

I have lived and worked here all my life, but forces of one sort and another have pulled me away every so often, to Baghdad and Karachi, Cairo and Istanbul, Jersusalem, Paris and London, Rome, Los Angeles, Moscow, Venice and Florence, Nice, New York and Milan. I have some affection for most of these great cities and what amounts to a true passion for some, but Edinburgh survives. It is a very special place to come home to.

It is my experience that the people I live with are narrow, diffident, conservative and wickedly proud—and warm, generous, independent of mind and tolerant. We cultivate eccentricity and buttress the status quo. We aspire to internationalism and make a monument out of the parish pump. We entice the world to our international festival of the arts and have yet to lay a single brick in its name.

"One word," says a clever advertisement, "is worth a thousand pictures." They were selling a camera with a famous name. But say "Edinburgh" to anyone who has been here and the images will tumble over each other like washing in a demented machine. Douglas Corrance has found a way to slow the thing down, select shapes and colours and textures on our behalf, and programme our minds to the right responses.

W. GORDON SMITH

9

The Castle is uncompromising. It is an international cliché, as instantly symbolic of Edinburgh as the Parthenon is of Athens. Yet it constantly defies the contempt of familiarity. Turn a corner, raise your head, glance in a mirror, catch a reflection, look up, see yonder, today it is different yet again, a backdrop for a Georgian cottage. Sometimes it is spiky and angular, perched on a precipice. Sometimes strangely elongated, laid low, slumbering. Never quite the sum of its ill-assorted parts. Never absolutely ugly. Dawn and dusk turn its flanks pink and pretty. Rain weeps off its walls and polishes the blackness of its volcanic pedestal. Hot twilights dust it lilac and purple. Hard frosts freeze it to the glitter of polar ice. It is diminished by sunshine.

 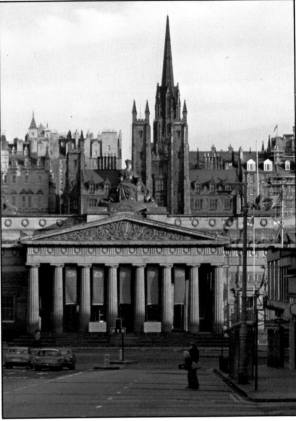

When Walter Scott was knighted in 1820 his servant Tom Purdie had the markings of the sheep at Abbotsford changed from "W.S." to "S.W.S.". There is a hint of this overweening pride in the monument to his master—George Kemp's incredible Gothic rocket—which awaits posterity's final countdown at the east end of Princes Street.

Playfair's classical façade for the Royal Scottish Academy, bannered in crimson and gold as if Hanover Street were a tributary of the Grand Canal. Beyond is The Mound, former midden, climbing to the spine of the old town—tenements, the square towers of New College and the hypodermic steeple of Tolbooth St John's.

It is bastion and stronghold, barracks and prison and head-quarters. It is museum and shrine, chapel and dog's cemetery. It is all of these things. And also a kind of grail or tabernacle, the high place on which the first people began to build their city where they were safe from wolves and could see the advance of their enemies.

St Giles' Cathedral, the High Kirk of Edinburgh, is the ecclesiastical heart of Scotland and the hub of much of the nation's history. The superb Chapel of the Most Noble Order of the Thistle is a modern addition, designed by Sir Robert Lorimer and built in 1911. Its carvings are the most ornate executed in Scotland since the Middle Ages.

Across a frozen putting-green, through a black filigree of budless branches, the city's masters and servants burn the afternoon oil in municipal offices ancient and modern. Above them, on the higher plateau of the High Street, the airy crown-steeple of St Giles' Cathedral rises rose-red, delicate in the winter air.

Edinburgh shares the same latitude as Moscow. There are days in every year
when it looks like it, weeks when it feels like it. And when driven snow turns
the garden slopes into a vast white canvas a flick of a switch conjures Santa
Claus and his reindeer—or anything else you fancy.

15

In a perfect world Charlotte Square and St Andrew Square would be identical, linked by the broad ribbon of George Street. As it is, Charlotte Square is an architectural jewel and St Andrew Square is a dog's breakfast. The north side of Charlotte Square is regarded as Robert Adam's masterpiece. It is that rare thing, an almost perfect composition, satisfying in its completeness, precise in its detail—solid without weight, lightness without frivolity. It is like a last movement by Mozart when the maestro pulls everything together and brings off another small miracle. No. 6 is Bute House, the official capital residence of the Secretary of State for Scotland. No. 7 is furnished and decorated as it might have been in the eighteenth century and is open to the public.

How very clever of the Scottish Arts Council to distort the image of a street lamp into a shape that would do justice to the pen of Charles Rennie Mackintosh. And one can almost see the inquiring eye of Mr MacFadyen behind his modern peephole while his nameplate reflects the opposite façade in Northumberland Street.

City soot and over a century of burnishing have pitted the surface of a door plate which, in its day, has reflected the passage of many stately coaches. Whereas the National Trust for Scotland, who would be right to regard the motor car as a threat to much that they protect, are stuck with it. Parked cars spoil every townscape. In Edinburgh they are calamitous.

Regrettably few people live today in Charlotte Square's magnificent Georgian houses. It is a commercial museum, a place for work and waiting for buses. There are many gibes about Edinburgh, the "penniless lass wi' a lang pedigree", jokes about kippers and pianos, and about the greeting you get on an Edinburgh doorstep, like "you'll have had your tea". Edinburghers are alleged to be east-windy and west-endy, a bit aloof, stand-offish, apt to keep their distance. It is nothing more than a whim of coincidence that the bus queue lends substance to that claim. And the lady sheltering alone while she awaits her No. 17 passes the time with a copy of Scotland's national comic paper.

There is more than one form of . . .

. . . municipal transport, isn't there?

An unkind opponent of conservation once said that Edinburgh had invented a new nervous disease, astragalitis, the chief symptom of which is an overwhelming and irrational need to replace perfectly sound single-pane modern windows with a dozen panes set in convex wooden mouldings, making cleaning an even greater chore and reducing the amount of available light. The Scottish Arts Council have their headquarters and gallery in Charlotte Square where the upper half of the ground floor windows are gracefully curved. Considering the cost of replacement it is as well that football is not a popular pastime in this neighbourhood.

A more conventional window gives out on to Saxe-Coburg Place, one of
several northern extremities of the New Town, which wandered away or were
separated from the grand plan. Other notable examples are Malta Terrace
and Warriston Crescent. All lie close to the Water of Leith. Saxe-Coburg
Place has the dignity and confinement of a square without actually being
one. Its houses are lived in, carefully preserved, and the residents enjoy a
detached and leafy serenity. As it happens they don't play much football here
either. But in many front rooms grand pianos are kept in tune.

Some places preserve railways or pub mirrors or old motor cars. Edinburgh, through the special interest of the local Co-op, still uses the working horse for milk deliveries in the central city. On special State occasions and during Edinburgh Festivals a common old working chap never knows who he'll have to share his stables with—a snooty drum horse of the Household Cavalry or some frisky foreign filly who keeps disgusting hours. Hilly Edinburgh, with so many hoof-splitting cobbles, is probably not the best place to be yoked to a cart of heavy milk crates. But there are compensations in the quiet curve of Bellevue Crescent, with the parish clock at twenty-to-eight, the sun just up, and the lady's put her slippers on to bring out some breakfast.

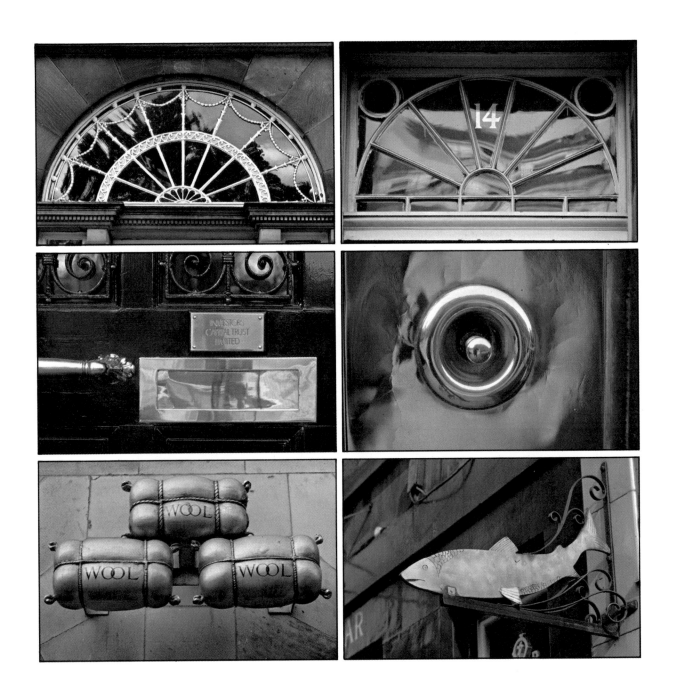

The genteel generation who went in for scalloped window-blinds wanted to keep the world away, to see yet not be seen, and they betrayed their curiosity only by a nervous tremor of rustled lace. They still keep their dramas to themselves, shutting out the sun, marking time in a sad twilight while the paint peels and the woodwork sags.

Another generation, other attitudes, brash, confident, enjoying a very public privacy. Lace curtains certainly, dark glasses too, but here comes the sun, and why not spread out a towel and use a sooty pillar for a pillow, and what else are city window-ledges for on a hot Sunday afternoon?

The hugger-mugger life of the Old Town tenements, the teeming high "lands" of the Lawnmarket and Canongate communities, died when reconstruction and slum clearance sent the folk out to the suburban wilderness. In some city enclaves, however, "back court" living survives against a backdrop of undressed brick, between clothes-poles and dark close-mouths. And against a more traditional texture of random rubble lucky tenement dwellers can still indulge the ancient pastime of "hingin' oot", a grandstand perch for the eternal passing show. "There's nothing like it," they'll assure you. "Better than the telly." And they'll be right.

The clash and crush of Princes Street is only yards away but there is usually a vacant bower here by the gardens, a happy trap for warmth and light and scented air, and quiet enough for a spicy crack with a friend or a relative or, better still, the complete stranger who moved along to let you rest your feet.

Outside the wind can be blowing
sleet in their ears. Fog has
swallowed the Calton Hill. The Water
of Leith changes from lazy snake to
roaring brown bear. But in the great
canopied hall of the Royal Scottish
Museum the climate stays steady,
milky light spills over everything,
and the only sound is the thrashing
of a frantic goldfish.

If the story of the Pied Piper had not been set in Hamelin it could have happened here, on an arcaded terrace warren above Victoria Street looking down on the Grassmarket. Sensible crows have not yet stepped on the snowy gables. Sounds are muffled. Hard edges soften and blur. Contrasts deepen between darker browns and paler pastels. The entire visible world seems cut out of cheese.

Victoria Street licked with bright paint and well on the way to complete rehabilitation, from dusty warehouses with eyeless windows to a self-energizing chain of craft shops, jewellers, old books, antiques, old clothes, good coffee, incredible brushes, a disco, a pub, and the annexe of the Sheriff Court. Not too transient. Not too static. Interesting.

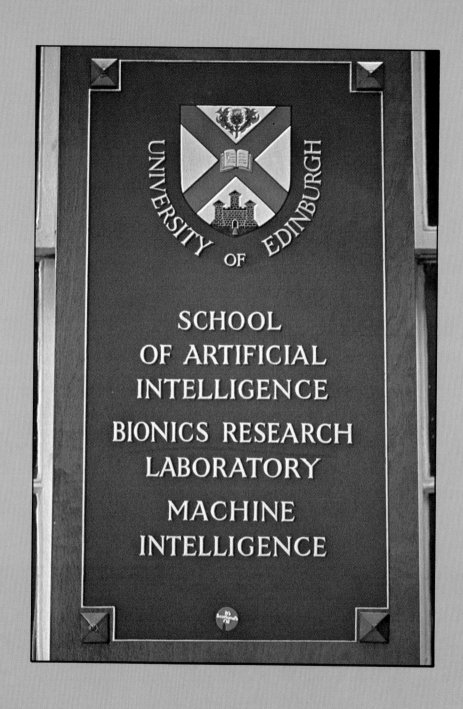

UNIVERSITY OF EDINBURGH

**SCHOOL
OF ARTIFICIAL
INTELLIGENCE**

**BIONICS RESEARCH
LABORATORY**

**MACHINE
INTELLIGENCE**

An ancient university, founded in 1582, moves towards its 400th birthday equipped with some of the ominous sciences of a brave new world. The slogan on the political sticker seems to suggest that some functions of the department are already redundant.

The full title is The Royal Repository for Gentlewomen's Work, and it lives in George Street and performs many good works in mysterious ways. Very Edinburgh. Other Scottish towns could support such a place but a Glasgow branch is unlikely.

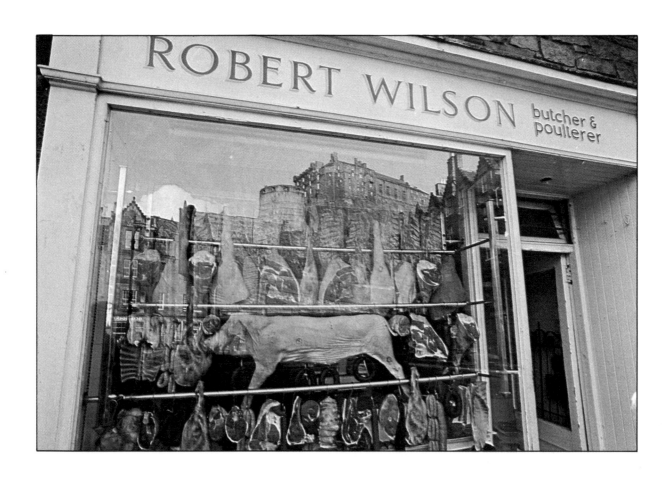

A very old West End grocery shop, the sort of place where they let you taste the cheese before you buy, where the claret still comes in wooden cases, where truffles and tinned wild boar are commonplace. One has the feeling that they would deliver two ounces of salami to a good customer, then forget to send in the bill. If they sniff when you ask for a tin of beans, they do it very quietly.

A very new secondhand bookshop in the West Port. In more leisurely days book collectors from all over the world came to plunder Edinburgh's shelves. A former Lord Provost wrote "The Diary of a Bankrupt Bookseller", but under a pseudonym. He was trying to tell us something. The trade has indeed dwindled. Or perhaps it has just gone underground.

Only Perth rivals Edinburgh in the variety and character of its antique shops. They range from plush to quaint, from junk shops whose stock looks as if it had been swept off the saleroom floor, to specialists in Oriental treasures, exquisite furniture, bijouterie, and precious carpets. Beyond the shop fronts pantechnicons are loaded with old pianos for Holland, Victorian monstrosities for New York, anything at all for Japan. The turnover is voracious. The sources, wherever they are, appear to be inexhaustible. Yet they cannot be unless, as a result of inflation, an international ring of dealers is moving the objects round the world in some awful circle. Is it possible that, after an economic miracle for us and disaster for everyone else, we might want to buy it all back?

The lady is a legend. So are her cats—never fewer than a dozen, say her neighbours. She is Madame Doubtfire, seller of old clothes for half a century from her shop near Stockbridge. The hat is rakish. The face is strong with a leathery tan. The eyes have seen and measured most things. The cat has probably seen more.

The bagpipe-maker of the Lawnmarket. His shop is howff and trysting-place for regiments of thirsty pipers. His workshop is a mess of ebonies and ivories, tartan bags and sheep's bladders, tasselled silks and cunning reeds, and mysterious tools which have been handed on as if they were part of a masonic ritual. Which indeed they are.

The shop is called "Violins Etc" but to most tradition-respecting Scots the instruments are fiddles, a distinction that even Yehudi Menuhin doesn't disagree with. Apart from reels and strathspeys which would set the toes of statues tapping, the slow melodic airs of Scott Skinner, with all their lambent passion, are part of the great folk music of the world.

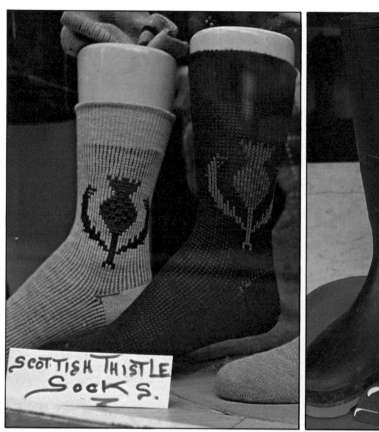

Opposite: If Harrods is representative of a kind of London, Jenners speaks
very eloquently for much of Edinburgh. The shop on Princes Street is a
landmark, its window displays are famous, and inside they find time to care
about the customer. The hammer-beamed grand hall, reminiscent of
Liberty's in London, was designed by William Hamilton Beattie and
completed in 1895.

No, not the audience chamber of an Arabian prince, nor the throne room at Holyrood, but the public banking hall of the Royal Bank of Scotland in St Andrew Square and worth a visit even if you want only the change of a pound. Far and away the most distinguished building in a square that has been sadly knocked about, the bank building began its life as a house for Sir Laurence Dundas. Sir William Chambers designed it in 1772, and his star-crusted dome is pierced by over a hundred shafts of cool northern light. St Andrew Square, incidentally, houses a disproportionate amount of the western world's wealth. Many great banking and insurance houses keep their computerized coffers under the 100-foot pillar dedicated to another Dundas, Viscount Melville.

The Bank of Scotland Head Office has less architectural merit but occupies one of the most commanding sites in the city, perched at the top of the Mound, offering views across the Forth to Fife and beyond. The bank was founded in 1695 and built these headquarters in 1806 to a design by Richard Crichton and Robert Reid. Sixty years later the building was reconstructed and extended by David Bryce. William of Orange was on the throne when the bank began, and the Act of the Scots Parliament by which it was constituted was one of 145 pieces of legislation passed that year, including an Act for a Solemn Fast, an Act against Profaneness, an Act in Favour of Periwig Makers, and an Act against Burying in Scots Linen.

Robert Adam's skeely hand draughted the design of Register House at the east end of Princes Street, but it was Robert Reid who completed its building between 1822 and 1827. This is the Scottish records office, the deed-box of the nation, housing historical and legal records, including wills, from the thirteenth century on.

Edinburgh is studded with memorials to Scotland's military prowess and shocking catalogue of war dead. This young infantryman, a King's Own Scottish Borderer, is part of a lively tableaux by Bernie Rhind unveiled in 1906 on the east side of North Bridge. The General Post Office lies beyond the black sheds of Waverley Station.

One route to the Castle, up the almost perpendicular Ramsay Lane, leads to Ramsay Gardens, an enclave of gabled and turreted houses hugging the hill like an Alpine settlement at the east end of the esplanade. Most of the houses are beautiful. Some—like Goosepie lodge, Allan Ramsay's last home—are eccentric. All are very expensive. And noisy when the massed pipes and drums of the Festival Tattoo make merry for a month every year.

The Royal Mile is the bent spine of old Edinburgh, running down a steep rocky ridge from the Castle to the Palace of Holyroodhouse, from Castle Hill through the Lawnmarket into the High Street and down the Canongate to the open meadows below Arthur's Seat. Much of the Lawnmarket has been, rebuilt or restored, keeping the character of the original tenement "lands" which gave Edinburgh the dubious distinction of erecting the first high-rise housing. Dank closes give out on to spacious quadrangles, or courts, as they are called. For the first half of this century they throbbed with the heartbeat of lusty communities who lived, for the most part, in deprived conditions. Today, out in the suburbs, the survivors remind each other how happy they were.

John Knox's House juts out over the cobbles just before the High Street becomes the Canongate. Many authorities believe that the great preacher, "father" of the Scottish Reformation and disciple of John Calvin, lived in this house from 1561 to 1572, that this was his manse when he was minister of St Giles'. It is only fair to record that this belief is hotly disputed. Nevertheless, the house is known to have been built in 1490 and is certainly one of the most attractive of Edinburgh's historic dwellings. Above all, it is known to be typical of much of the old town, and its pretty timbered galleries, once a common feature of the skyline, are the sole remaining examples. A stern reminder of how much has been lost.

Every member of the Faculty of Advocates has a wooden box, with a brass nameplate and a lock, stacked in a corridor in the precincts of the Courts of Justice at Parliament House, close to St Giles' Cathedral. When the Courts are sitting men go to the houses or chambers of the advocates every morning, "bag" all the relevant papers for that day's cases and bring them to the boxes. The procedure is reversed in the evenings. An ancient custom, and an honourable one, because although the boxes have locks there are no keys. And the corridor is unguarded. Such is the profession's trust in its membership that vital confidential information, upon which the outcome of a civil action might hang, could lie alongside the papers of an opposing counsel.

Parliament Hall is reputed to have the finest hammer-beam roof north of the Tweed. It is now the waiting-hall of Scotland's supreme courts, civil and criminal, the Court of Session and the High Court. In session time it is thronged with advocates in wig and gown, promenading and posturing and gesticulating as they worry away at case details with solicitors and clients. The large pictorial window of Munich glass at the south end, where the throne used to stand, depicts the institution of the Court of Session by James V in 1532. Portraits of wise judges and passionate pleaders ruminate in a heavy silence. One resists the temptation to make these noble rafters ring with a great shout.

The Palace of Holyroodhouse has been knocked about so much that it lacks any convincing unity. A recent scouring of its old stones, however, has certainly put a better face on things and it has even been seen to sparkle on a summer day. Built originally by James IV and James V, sacked, burned and bashed, it has survived somehow. After James VI took his court to London the palace's importance waned. Victoria stopped off occasionally on her way to Balmoral. Edward VII lodged here while studying in Edinburgh. His successors have braved the draughty interior on a regular basis. The true mistress of Holyrood was Mary Queen of Scots. Her romantic sadness has seeped into its walls. She danced, cried, laughed, saw murder done, married, and met failure here at Holyrood.

"Eyes Left!" as members of the Royal Company of Archers dress their parade. The command is as politically inappropriate to a body of "noblemen and gentlemen of good social position" as their bows and arrows are anachronistic in an age of Armalite rifles and rubber bullets. Formally adopted as the monarch's bodyguard in Scotland by George IV in 1822, the Archers have significant rights of precedence as well as a most picturesque ceremonial garb. They wear something simpler for shooting. Predominantly middle-aged, they are a company of about 500 men commanded by a captain-general. They shoot regularly at the butts and compete for annual prizes. And when the sovereign takes up residence at Holyrood they fall in and mount guard, provide colourful escort, and act as getlemen-in-waiting.

Ceremonial is something more than ritual and show in a capital city. Trusts are honoured, allegiance is shown in an intricate web that is part of the fabric of a nation. And there are different ways to be suitably dressed for the occasion—in this case an installation ceremony of the Most Ancient and Most Noble Order of the Thistle.

If you cut any kind of physical dash and have the confidence to wear it with just the right blend of poise and swagger there is all the pride of the peacock in a gentleman's Highland evening dress. Many outfits go as far as frothy lace jabots and cuffs and perforated dancing pumps laced to the calves. Ladies settle for less.

In a city of violent contrasts there is none so startling as the possibility of quitting the hubbub of Princes Street and within minutes finding oneself in a miniature Highland landscape of mountain, lochs and glen—the Queen's Park, Arthur's Seat, Dunsappie Loch, Salisbury Crags, St Margaret's Loch, and the strangely sinister ruin of St Anthony's Chapel. From the top of Arthur's Seat much of lowland Scotland rolls away towards the hills of Perthshire in the north and Berwick Law to the east. One can see the city, sense its heartbeat but hear none of its din. The deep pastoral calm is broken only by the munching of grass or what Robert Louis Stevenson called "the whispering rumour of a train".

If your excuse for a walk is feeding ducks, chimpanzees, geese, pigeons,
polar bears or milk horses, Edinburgh offers ample scope, but not all in the
same place and certainly not all in the Queen's Park. Here the Queen's peace
is properly kept for Her Majesty and her lieges and all wild things. A road runs
through the park but traffic is restricted to a crawl. The only danger is the
possibility of being trampled to death by joggers.

Edinburghers enjoy more of the qualities of life than most city dwellers, which is perhaps why, over the past half-century, they have neglected the beach and other amenities of Portobello, a natural seaside resort, lapping on their doorstep. They have looked askance at Welsh rugby supporters who camp out for a week by the sea on their bi-annual pilgrimage to Murrayfield. Before Glaswegians conquered the costas of Spain they claimed Portobello as their own while their Eastern cousins sniffed in disdain. And complained about thin sand, cold winds, the absence of facilities, dirty water and (so long as the power-station chimney still stood) the smuttiest sun tans in Britain. But fishermen love it in winter and small boys and retrieving dogs seem contented there all the time.

There is no archetypal Scot. They come in all shapes and sizes, lots of fair ones, many dark ones, some tall ones, more short ones, and not so many wee bandy ones as there used to be. But for the personification of a very special kind of Scot—ginger-haired, freckled, bright-eyed, arch mischief-maker—will this one do?

Or consider if you will this quartet outside a famous pub in the fishing village of Newhaven. They know all about catching partans and podlies, they're probably Hibernian supporters, and no matter where they end up in the lives before them they will never get the smell of the sea out of their noses or forget the adventure it promised.

Conservation goes on at Newhaven
but too much has been allowed to
go too far. The old villagers kept
themselves to themselves, marrying
within their own boundaries and
maintaining a legend of daring men
and strong women. Their houses
often echoed their Dutch or Danish
origins, with quaint gables and
attractive outside stairs. Some still
survive.

Edinburgh, or Auld Reekie as she was known in smokier times, swallowed up the great port of Leith in 1920—and surviving Leithers still curse the day it happened. Depopulation through slum clearance and higher living standards has drained the place of much of its robust and salty character. But big ships still come and go from the busy seaport.

Fishing harbours and the work that goes on in them have an endless fascination for the strollers and others with time to stand and stare. Newhaven offers shelter to pleasure craft as well as working boats so there is a hint of sleepy activity most of the time. Hammers bang, saws rasp, but the lap of gentle water muffles all.

It is no accident that Stevenson found his model for Jekyll and Hyde in a bent Edinburgh worthy. And the metaphor for good and bad, light and shade, rough and smooth, one thing by night and another by day can be applied with equal vigour to the modern city. Edinburgh can play Cinderella and Ugly Sister at the same time.

The city has many lungs—spacious suburban parks, the wide floral valley of
Princes Street Gardens, four miles of rolling pasture round Arthur's Seat,
and the cleverly planned private gardens of the New Town, oases of grass
and trees and sooty shrubbery. They belong to the nearby householders
who maintain them in good condition and keep the public out with high
fences and locked gates. Wartime experience of open access suggested that
restrictions were necessary, no matter how regrettable. In spring and
summer they are the playparks of children, lucky enough not to use the
streets, and their basking mums. In winter the bushes drip in forlorn gloom
until the snow comes. Autumn brings its own alchemy. Smoke from burning
leaves and milky November light turn Royal Circus into a Gothic woodland
glade.

The Royal Botanic Garden, to the north of the city centre, is remarkable for what it sets out to be, a cold-climate Kew, a repository for superb botanical specimens from all over the world, many of them perforce under glass. But it is from the "Botanics", as they are popularly called, and particularly from the vantage point of the magnificent rock garden, that one sees the best possible panorama of the city skyline. And set in the heart of the park, on what is proving to be a long-term "temporary" basis, is the Scottish National Gallery of Modern Art. For the moment one arboreal specimen is receiving more attention than the sculpture of Barbara Hepworth. And Henry Moore and Reg Butler may fare no better.

Less than five minutes' walk from the west end of Princes Street, under Telford's towering bridge, down in the deep gorge of the Water of Leith, a miracle of urban life—the hamlet of Dean. The Well Court, clock tower and all, looks like something Walt Disney might have created for "Pinocchio". In fact it is a complex of small flats. Alongside runs Edinburgh's river, often no more than a stream, but clear and sparkling and well enough stocked with trout to offer reasonable sport. Most of the restoration of the Dean Village reflects nothing but credit on the good taste and workmanship of architects and craftsmen who obviously respected the merits of traditional Scottish domestic buildings.

Salesmen of the city's sunny merits have been known to break down and cry at the prospect of a photograph like this appearing in a book like this. But many a weary citizen, homeward bound on a January afternoon, sprayed by the slush from hissing tyres, has seen the towers of Daniel Stewart's-Melville College poking up through lentil soup.

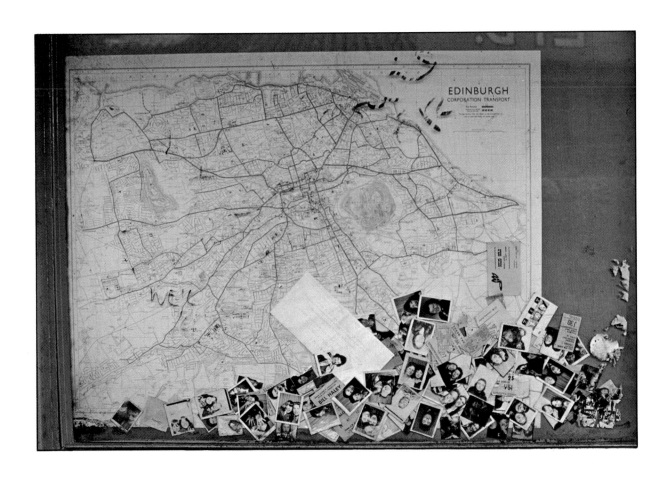

How did it start? Where will it end? A chink in the frame of a city map at a bus shelter. Someone drops in the ticket for a pop concert, someone else adds a photograph. Soon photographs are being taken only for this purpose. And in no time at all a random collage is created, saying "we have been here".

The clock stands at a quarter past three, there's a while to go before they serve tea, and a sore back is a sore back wherever you are, especially on a steamy sports day at Donaldson's School for the Deaf, Playfair's splendid edifice just beyond Haymarket. One of many schools in the city which were generously endowed by local philanthropists.

In the eighteenth century Edinburgh gentry promenaded in the grounds of George Heriot's School, originally gifted for the education of the sons of poor freemen, now a fee-paying day school. Cromwell used this fascinating building as a military hospital. Heriot, jeweller and banker to James VI, was the original of Scott's Jingling Geordie in "The Fortunes of Nigel".

Matchstick boys, red-legged like oyster-catchers, peck about on the snowy terraces in front of Daniel Stewart's-Melville College. Like all boys they are impervious to the cold as they choose targets for the next salvo of snowballs, unconscious of the shapes they make in a white world, oblivious to the inevitable comparisons with the work of L. S. Lowry.

If you stage a free-and-easy festival
in the Meadows, once a loch now a
jealously preserved park, you
shouldn't be surprised if a miniature
Pancho Villa draws his pistol on the
pipers. "Under these trees," wrote
Lord Cockburn, "walked and talked
and meditated all our literary and
scientific worthies."

During the Edinburgh Festival a morning piper entertains the Princes Street throng at the base of the Scott Monument. They come in all sizes from far and near these members of one of the world's most exclusive fraternities. The degree of virtuosity varies. Some have led armies, others only haggises. An unquenchable thirst is their most endearing common characteristic.

A gangrel group of wooden puppets at their suspended ease in the Museum of Childhood, one of the pure joys of Edinburgh, offering total enchantment on wet day or dry. There is everything from Victorian dolls to antique stink-bombs, eccentric clockwork toys to macabre working models, peep-shows, flying machines, nursery purgatives, and jokes for the sadistic prankster.

White Horse Close, at the foot of the Canongate, housed the inn from which the coach for London usually departed in the good old days. Its reconstruction in 1962 left it looking as if a chorus of maidens and swineherds would, at the drop of a golden guinea, spring from the shadows and perform a musical comedy.

In an age of ton-up motor-cycles, express elevators, skateboards, ski-jumps and hang-gliding, one would think that the need to scare oneself to death at the fairground would have diminished or disappeared. But showmen keep coming to the Meadows in their gay caravans and look as if the spectre of Social Security is a long way off.

Out in the fields it would be suitably matted by wind and weather, or parted daily on a convenient fence-post or tree. But the coiffure of an aristocratic Highland beast at the Royal Highland Show must be dressed according to the best traditions for the presentation of pedigree cattle. And he can still see you, don't ever forget it!

In spring and autumn when the sun hangs low in the sky the character of Edinburgh is dramatically changed by heavy sidelighting, as if punched on to a stage setting from the wings. Textures are revealed, contours enhanced, contrasts deepened, and the dip and rise of the townscape melts away into smoky glimpses of sea or hills not far away.

Commercial boldness versus aesthetic discretion. A butcher proclaims his wares with colourful conviction. The brass plate outside No. 17 Heriot Row, Stevenson's boyhood home, sighs gently. There is still a lamp before the door but unromantic bureaucracy decrees that the light should nowadays come from electric filament instead of gas mantle. Alas, poor Leerie!

There is an unequivocal brusqueness about the door bell in its black and forbidding frame. But by the same token the red door extends a warm welcome. Puritanical conservationists, of which there are many, would probably ignore the former and deplore the latter. The lamp is the standard approved lantern for the New Town. On a black night they sparkle like baubles.

Only grain whisky is distilled in Edinburgh, but hundreds of thousands of gallons of malt and grain whiskies lie in bonded warehouses for many years, awaiting maturity and the subtle skills of the blender. Whisky in bond represents millions of unpaid pounds to the Exchequer. Duty is not paid until the mature spirit leaves the warehouse prior to blending and bottling. Until then H.M. Customs and Excise take a diligent interest in the security of the bond and the level of spirit in the barrels. The old warehouses, like Crawford's at Leith, are as impregnable as medieval keeps—double padlocks, barred windows and all. New bonds, herded together like eyeless monsters, litter the countryside all over Lowland Scotland, representing a potential value that would challenge the wealth of Fort Knox.

The reputation of Scottish pubs was earned in the dour days of sawdust floors and the kind of cheerless dedicated drinking that sought swift oblivion and nothing else. Zealous drinkers the Scots remain, as statistics testify, but now topless go-go dancers are not unknown amongst the drams and wee heavies. Edinburgh has several notable Victorian pubs of character and good cheer as well as a quota of the unspeakable chrome and plastic conversions. The old pubs keep their regular customers and attract new ones by that ancient formula compounded of cluttered decor, attentive service, fellowship, good beer, fair measures and a smiling barmaid. And in these days of miraculously relaxed licensing laws, who cares if the clock above the bar stands permanently at midday? Or is it midnight?

He'll remember pale ale when it came in tall green screwtop bottles with a red rubber collar to keep the fizz in, light years before green cans and cunning aluminium ring-pulls. A pub for artisans of the Industrial Revolution near Haymarket, with celebratory stained-glass, scrubbed table-tops, dominoes chapping, and beer you could taste, pulled up fresh and lively from wooden barrels in the cellars by manual pumps and none of your rubbishy, artificially-induced CO_2 from cold metal canisters. And spirits? Half-a-crown a bottle before Lloyd George started to put the tax on it. Cheaper than half-a-crown in some places, where you could get an ounce of tobacco and some matches and a halfpenny change for your hard-earned 12½p. And they call it progress!

The man with the magnificent beard has a public platform—at the Speaker's Corner of the north, the Mound on a Sunday p.m. And he has a passion, as his poster and his posture proclaim. It is only right and proper, in a city of reactionary reputation, that his only audience should look at best sceptical, at most downright underwhelmed.

Easing even further beyond the pale, a Communist Party rally skirts the very flanks of the Castle Rock, aiming at the city's heart. Youth is on the march. Their banners are unambiguous. And a senior citizen, complete with shopping bag, left fist clenched in sisterly fervour, adds the weight of her years and disillusionment to the protestations of the young.

At first sight, hockey, on the broad plateau of Ferry Road on a northern rise between the Castle and the Firth of Forth. And a boot inspection for wayward nails or ragged studs. Then a closer look at the sticks and these goalposts. Shinty. A Highland game with a wild reputation. Uninhibited hockey. The Scottish equivalent of Irish hurling. A man's game. And, as legend has it, a drinking man's game in which the mileage covered and energy expired is directly related to the amount of malt whisky consumed between matches. At any rate, shinty, with curling, is one of the few honestly indigenous Scottish games. The world quarrels about where golf started, but there are no arguments—at least not that kind of argument—about shinty.

There is a brewery less than a quarter of a mile away, industrial smoke still belching, and the main railway line to London just beyond the gates, but with a willing pony under you, the going good, and some friends to join you in a gallop, you could be riding the marches of a Border dale instead of Queen's Park.

Inverleith Park has facilities for many sports—from tennis to catching sticklebacks, bowls, cricket, model boating, rugby, duck-feeding, and soccer. Heart of Midlothian, Hibernian and Meadowbank Thistle are the city's professional teams and they have loyal support despite the dominance of the great Glasgow teams. At Inverleith—and at Glasgow parks too—they'll tell you that their football is best.

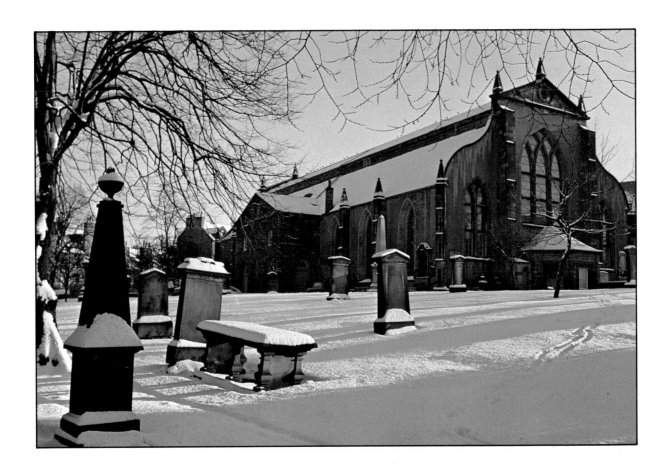

Greyfriars Churchyard has a special place in Scotland's history, and not because of the faithful terrier, Greyfriars Bobby, whose devotion to his dead master made him one of the most famous dogs in the world. Bobby is buried at Greyfriars and his memorial fountain is just across the road on George IV Bridge. But the significance of the old kirkyard is its connection with the Covenanters. The National Covenant was signed here—sometimes in blood—in 1638, and after the Battle of Bothwell Bridge in 1679, 1200 Covenanters were held prisoner in the open yard, rigorously guarded and poorly fed. Greyfriars is the resting-place of many notable Scots, and the old church, much altered since it was built in 1614, sports copies of the Covenanters' flags.

Because of global transmissions of television programmes the image of Edinburgh best known to countless millions of people is the searchlit esplanade of the Castle during the Festival Tattoo. And for thousands of capital citizens all they have ever seen of the annual jamboree of music and drama is the parade and musical pageant in this dramatic amphitheatre high above the town. The Tattoo has become a folk-festival in its own right and a huge box-office success. If the Glyndebourne ritual suggests long frocks and sunny picnics of champagne and smoked salmon sandwiches, the Tattoo drill involves tartan travelling rugs, plastic cushions, flasks of hot soup and corned beef rolls. And libations of that amber dew which banisheth all cold are not unknown.

Much of the Tattoo music is played on the bagpipes—massed bands and solitary lamenters, famous Highland regiments and little Gurkha riflemen who march and pipe quicker than anyone else. But one might also hear Breton bombards and wild Arabian bugles in between the big boom of military bands. The esplanade becomes a cockpit of chauvinist fervour. Waves of colour ebb and flow with immaculate precision. Commands and rifle butts rattle in the night air. Ranks form, advance, wheel, dissolve and miraculously form again in another geometric puzzle. Eccentric drill squads from foreign fields are graciously applauded. Historical charades are blown good-humoured raspberries. Ceremonial guardsmen from Turkey, Italy and France get wolf-whistles. And the English are gently teased until the great tartan tide sweeps all before it.

The Adam family—William and his
sons, John and Robert—and Sir
William Bruce all had a hand in
creating Hopetoun House, the
magnificent mansion of the
Marquess of Linlithgow, a genuinely
stately home beyond South
Queensferry. A suitable setting for
Rembrandt and Rubens and
Raeburn, and for the recitals of
chamber music which have drawn
new admirers to Hopetoun.

Festivals are about many things—
about joy and excellence, about
experiment and the constant
reiteration of that which has been
proved to be special. They are also
about friendship, the linking of
peoples and cultures, and the
reunion of mere men like Leonard
Bernstein and Peter Diamand,
maestro and entrepreneur.

So there I was at this bizarre Festival exhibition of . . . well, they called it
tapestry . . . anyway, I'd just got around this "thing" and who do you think?
That nice little man on the telly, the conductor, Andre Preview, as Eric
Morecambe calls him. He seemed bemused, too, but the Lord Provost
looked as if he knew what he liked.

The infectious exuberance of Daniel Barenboim is obvious enough in performance, whether he is playing or conducting. There he is, rehearsing for a performance, relishing the challenge of a particularly daunting passage, and at tea break he is out in the sun with his friends, perfectly balanced, eyes on the ball, boring in on goal, presto furioso.

Because there is nowhere to mount it, classical ballet gets practically no
representation at the Festival. So the stage has been clear for small modern
dance teams, many of which come from abroad, like this group from the
United States.

"Don Giovanni" at the King's Theatre which can manage Mozart but not grand opera without serious technical compression. It looks as if the much-promised opera house will only be built by what insurance people call an Act of God.

If it's true that there would be no Festival Fringe without the existence of the official Festival, it is equally true that the annual beano would be a dull affair without the contribution of the hundreds of actors, singers and dancers who bring wit, vitality, invention, vulgarity, and often work of the highest quality to the greyer shores of art. They come from every continent, amateurs and professionals, the sponsored and penniless, the talented and the merely extravert. The Fringe has provided shaky platforms for artists who are now amongst the world's greatest performers, and consigned others to oblivion. This group of actors from Poland enhanced an already significant international reputation by performing in a former municipal poorhouse overlooking Greyfriars churchyard. That's about par for the Festival Fringe course.

Great virtuoso performers like Isaac Stern come to Edinburgh to express opinions as well as work and play. The morning press conferences are usually lively, often controversial, sometimes highly diverting. It is a time for trailing coats, flying kites, biting the feeding hand, and stuffing the critics' words up their nostrils. Another form of free expression is the Traverse Tattoo, a sort of artistic go-as-you-please, staged in the courtyard of the Traverse Theatre. In and out of Festival time the Traverse continues to justify its good name as a progressive modern theatre, encouraging new writing and producing a few brilliant young directors. The lady with all the jewellery is clearly enjoying herself. She has the air of someone who knows precisely what festivals ought to be about.

Another sumptuous setting for baroque music—the library of the Society of Writers to the Signet, an association of Scottish solicitors, which occupies the east side of Parliament Square. It was built in 1815. The Scottish Baroque Ensemble, a gifted chamber group, are playing in the fine upper hall of the library which is as richly ornamented as their music.

There is nothing baroque but much that is ornamental in the music of the fiddler's rally, a comparatively recent and immensely successful phenomenon in popular entertainment. They fill the Usher Hall with the swinging rhythms of jigs and reels, and the concerted din of 3000 pairs of feet tapping and hands clapping is almost enough to bring down the building.

Baleful Stare 1: I know what you all
think of us. I can hear you from here.
Gestapo. The Yellow Peril. Pigs. And
worse. But we've got a job to do and
at least our mothers love us. You
don't go out of your way to disguise
your feelings, do you? Well, I've got
news for you. I don't care!

Baleful Stare 2: I'd be very careful if I were you. I'm on duty, keeping the Queen's peace. That lot behind me are happy enough at the moment, but maybe they don't like being photographed either. Tell you what, let me know where you're working on my next day off, and I'll bring my Instamatic, and just when you're . . .

Baleful Stare 3: Look here, laddie, some of yon Red Indians wouldn't allow photographers near them because they believed the camera stole a part of their person. Now I'm not a Red Indian, as you can see. And I know that contraption of yours is harmless. But there's the small matter of a modelling fee. Would a fiver be all right with you?

East of Scotland travellers wax nostalgic about the charm and quaintness of the old car ferries that plied between North and South Queensferry. They forget the queues that used to add hours to the shortest journey during the tourist season. The Forth Road Bridge, which was opened in 1964, made the ferries redundant and transformed life in this corner of Scotland. Fife feels less like an island. Social life spills over to both sides of the estuary. There are deeper and wider commercial and industrial connections. And on top of all that, the bridge itself is beautiful, a graceful concrete arc that spans a mile of water in one effortless leap. There are two carriageways, two cycle tracks, and two footpaths. It cost almost £20 million to build.

The original Forth Bridge, exclusively for railway traffic, is as recognizable a Scottish symbol as the thistle. It was one of the engineering wonders of the world when it opened in 1890 and so it remains—massive yet delicate, beautiful in its awesome symmetry. The job of painting its 135 acres of vulnerable steel never ends. Five thousand men built it, using 54,000 tons of steel and 6½ million rivets. It cost £2¾ million. While it is always exciting to cross it in a train and cast a copper or two out of the window for luck, the demise of the ferries deprived most people of the best view of the bridge. At sea level, under its central span, the scale of the structure is breathtaking. Long may it survive.

Sir Compton Mackenzie once said
that he could tolerate Edinburgh's
winters but not her summers. So
long as the Siberian east wind is not
wheepling up the Forth, the city, and
especially its conserved open
spaces, suits a mantle of snow. Only
the birds at Duddingston could
complain. They may soon have to
give way to skaters.

Swanston village, "atween the muckle Pentland knees", was dearly loved by Robert Louis Stevenson as his holiday home. He spent much of his boyhood here among his "hills of home", guddling trout in the burns, living simply in a small thatched cottage. Even in Samoa, almost with his last breath, he pined for this place and blessed its airy serenity.

Nestled into a hollow at the base of the Castle Rock, the Grassmarket—
hunting-ground of Burke and Hare, a setting for circuses and riots, site of the
town gallows. Beyond the bleak winter trees festooned with fairy lights, a
dentifrice castle. As the sky darkens it will turn bright silver, float and defy
gravity in all its senses.